Piggy Bank

Piggy Bank

by Jacob Rubin

Gold Wake Press

Copyright © 2023 by Jacob Rubin. All rights reserved.

ISBN: 978-1-7377808-5-4

Published by Gold Wake Press

Cover design by Kevin Stone

No part of this book may be reproduced without permission from the author except in brief quotations and in reviews.

goldwake.com

for my sister, Nathania

CONTENTS

My Late Twenties	3
Burbank	5
Dave Made His Album	7
White Rock	9
My Flourishing Practice	11
Oedipus at Colonus	13
Diane's Keys	20
Kiss	26
Movies	28
Desert Surface #1	34
The Glass-Bottom Boat	39
God Is Sexting Me	41
To Denis Johnson	42
Aaron Judge	44
Blind Spot	45
Abundance	46
Samantha, the Dentist	47
To Albert Ayler	48
Bartleby's Diet	50
Pebbled Lips	51
Nick in the Video Room	53
To Pema Chodron	54
Double Indemnity	56

Notes
Acknowledgments
About the Author

My Late Twenties

The woman I fell in with
sawed off my wrists.
That map of her steps
on original floors,
the swooning corners
to which we repaired, etc.

At the office on 86th where the Xerox
could be heard from every room;
on that metal bench where I used to study
the East River's bovine passage,
I did some of my best thinking.

Once, during therapy, a moth appeared
in the cone of the lamp, and armed
with no more than his hand
and a hardback book,
the therapist ushered this lost insect
into a little courtyard
the office opened onto
through a dreamy back door.

I was all
turned around.

After the woman it was a downtown man
who liked to slice at my nose.
On and on it went in bars
where the bottles are lit from below
like camp counselors reciting ghost stories.

But things are less that way

when I remember
whose body is mine.
Just yesterday, in the salad
of the meadow,
my breath was the hand,
the ground, the book.

Burbank

Paisley incantations, email haiku,
and the golden Muzak of ten a.m.
feathering the rattling bursts of red hydrangea…

In a pitch room where a phone sat
in the middle of an oblong table,
my reflection in the window of canyons
looked to me like a passionate actor
who plays a vampire
in a $10 haunted house.

I have been back East for three years.
I'm glad I made the switch.
Advertising is at least coherent.
And I had missed the seasons.

When I remember being West,
the time is an empty aquarium.
Then a jellyfish floats by, and another,
with drifting independence:

The ocean, a salty screensaver.

Men whose pomegranate faces
had been bitten into by the sun,
wandered down Rose Avenue,
toting bulbous black garbage bags.

Giant posters loomed
behind gray-haired producers in jeans.

A month ago, I was watching
the Thanksgiving Day parade
from someone's two-bedroom.

Orange juice in little plastic cups.
Lox, bialys, and Goofy
soaring over Central Park West
with tiny people underneath him.

Dave Made His Album

Yellow of cheap OJ,
the winter sun went weakly
over bare branches.

In a blue Thinsulate coat,
the man on the Riverside bench
had a brown paper bag next to him
that leaned a little like a teddy bear.

As I got closer, I saw
it was my old friend
Dave.

I used to play a little
music with Dave. He would bang
on the wooden desk
as I sang in our dorm.

Being with him was
like sitting
by the ocean.

That day in December
I said hello, but over
a smile, his eyes
didn't know who I was.

Later, I heard Dave was living
in an empty warehouse.
Four years after Riverside,
I saw him at a party in a yard.
He was drinking seltzer, emitting
little polite clouds of inquiry.

Then an email came, saying
Dave was making an album.
Those who contributed ten bucks
would get a CD.

In Indio, California,
where the large and disgusting hills
are the color of desert camo,
I inserted the disc
into the player in my car.
The songs could be called soul
with bolts of harmony
poured like Skittles
into your hand.

Indio was smoky.
All summer, forests
had burned and Dave
had made his album.

White Rock

I was waiting at the drive-thru
when grandma flew in
through the window
of my Accord.

It took me a minute
to recognize her
due to the fact that
she was a dragonfly.

I said, Grandma Shelley!
She said, oh, it's you, Caleb.

I said, what are the chances?
I'm not sure, she said. I go over
to the enormous lake where I hear a noise
that must be a boat.

I said, White Rock?
She said, yeah. A lot of flies and midges there.

What does a fly taste like? I asked.
Like deep-fried black silk, she said.

Nice, I told her. Maybe I'll see you
there. I go pretty often
to look at the herons and beavers.

Maybe, she said. But I doubt it.

Last summer, a hound in a picture
window in Portland, ME,

was revealed to be Izzie,
the grandfather whom I knew
from late afternoons amid
plastic-covered couches
now madly barking
in a language of licking love.

And in California, Aunt Bessie
was a wobbly toddler
cheering like some crazed devotee
at a marathon's end.

What is going on?
Why is life so soft and fatal?
How come there's nowhere to go,
and yet we must survive?

It's okay, the dragonfly said.
Why don't you put up that photo
of me in my wedding dress
on the living room wall
and cook up a big russet stew?

And it flew away.

My Flourishing Practice

It was like trying to discern
the cry of a whale
in a cloudy blue surround
when I laid the stethoscope
upon a boy's pigeon chest.

The children, beatific germs
in little brown corduroy.

In my class in Cambridge, not many of us had religion,
and those who loved Christ
tended to support the president
who looked like a dissembling mortician
when he came on television
to talk about the war,
so I could never descry what others mean
by a word like "community,"
though I had colleagues and paramours,
like everyone else.

I couldn't make sense of Boston either,
being from the familial humidity of Virginia.
In the evenings, the tram looked
like a painting of an old saloon
being gradually moved across town.
The winters were minerals.

But I have been in Somerville
forty years, and my shadow
has traveled across my home,
like a watch I store
here and then there.

Standing before the mirror,
I see gray hair, a thin neck…

Why should she have been my favorite?
Why is having one like a sin?

A young woman
with what turned out to be appendicitis
was wheeled in at Mass General.
Back when I was doing my rounds.

The nerves made her eyes
even more wordless.
When I drove the needle in,
she laid her hand on my arm,
and we looked at each other.

Oedipus at Colonus

That day in West Hampton you and I were watching *Maury*
from the rattan couch
that had plums and apples
on its old white covers.

I'm sure you went out,
but in my memories
that's where you are:
in front of the television

because, from that spot,
you could keep an eye on the room
which I'm now really remembering.
The folk paintings of clapboard houses hung
over the mantel and beyond
the sliding doors, the lawn
where Ruby used to prance
with that log in her mouth.

That house carried the scent
of dust, sunlight, and cloth.
And in the plastic thing next
to the toilet on the second floor
lay the stack of *Playboys* where
a woman positioned on the lip
of a white hot tub
opened her heart chakra.

Grandma that day was upstairs,
or out
raking leaves.

You had a strong and square body
and thin, splayed legs
that were in white pants hiked to the calf.

By eight, I knew if I kept quiet,
the hooks in your words
could not find me.
That strategy was ok
though it also prevented me
from liking you.

Maury that afternoon
had on
prostitutes.

You, before my time, had appeared
on shows like that
where you spoke about real love
and dieting. In the short clips I've seen of *Donahue*,
you are like some enormous armchair
it would take at least two strong men
to get through a door.

You spent so much time going on
about the plight of the Jews.

It never really came up
that your own father
had been shot and killed

in Minsk,

a murder that must have had
something to do
with your boredom.

Boredom being like stillness
but with some little red troll
going crazy inside it.

In the one photo I've seen of your father,
he stands the way you used to.
The weight resides in the balls of his feet.
He wears a baggy, short-sleeved shirt and wool trousers.

I am told your father's friend later killed
the man who did it,
and you took Dad, when he was a child,
to meet the avenging semi-relative
in California.

I'm now a certified medical intuitive, btw.
When I close my eyes, I see the physical truth:
that your perineum could not relax, for instance,
because high up, along our etheric latticework
a gun is going off.

You would have really let me have it
for saying that.

We had that one big fight
about God,
on 110th.

Your famous rage
was like the violet exterior
of a Nissan Altima
I would later purchase from
an Addison dealership
in that it was a substance

that could turn hot or cold
and still be itself.

I think of you
while I drive.

I was thinking of you, too,
because of a literary idea I had relating
to an omission of Freud's:
namely, the whole thing with Oedipus
started when Laius heard a prophecy
that his newborn would kill him,
so the king shackled the baby's feet
and went up to Mount Cithaeron
and left the prince there.

But the gods can't be fooled.
So, a shepherd found the boy,
and Oedipus survived and went on
and later ingeniously solved
the Sphinx's riddle.

Meaning, Freud pinned the blame
of florid fantasies
on the child,
rather than even mentioning
what his father,
a grown man, had done.

Though, I can imagine why
Freud would side
with the parents:
babies have no money
and need a lot of help.

The parents have the crown, etc.,
and Oedipus is just some baby
freaking out in the mountains.

But still,

I think you would have agreed
that is a major omission

and then you would have turned
to the television.

The other day, I was reading
Oedipus at Colonus,
which is not as good
as *Rex* is.

The plot is that
Oedipus wanders in the direction of Athens
in pursuit of a premonition.

Everywhere the blind king goes people gape
at the horror
that pools around him
like a sable robe.

But Athens' king cares for Oedipus
more than most anyone in Thebes
did. And the gods,
the riddle solver's former tormentors,
now point like loyal dogs
to the grove of laurel and olive
where the worn man can rest.

What's more,
Oedipus knows the truth.
I mean,
he's had time to think.

I had been wronged, he says, *I retaliated;*
even had I known
what I was doing, was that evil?
Then, knowing nothing, I went on. Went on…

I think that's really
beautiful because
in my experience
it is like that
in this place where I still am,
but you have departed,
where the Gods, like the scent of cinnamon, are real
but invisible,
and walking down the honest path
feels like
having no eyes.

I hear you now when I light the blue candle
and receive you on
what my training calls
the cordless phone. Your voice boils
with our living blood
when you pledge your love to me.

That day in West Hampton, you muted *Maury,*
and said, "That's the only honest profession.
Everyone does the same thing,
but prostitutes are the only ones
who are honest about it."

Why can't I believe that?

I love you now.
I am free to ask.

And how come
when we abandon the baby
in the cold mountain
with shackled feet,
he always comes back?

Diane's Keys

Abe scampers in from the terrace excited to report that the top of his building can be seen from out there. He's wearing that Merino wool sweater his new stepmom got him and looks kind of good in it, but in this wack Euro way.

"Why is seeing your building an event, exactly?" Justin, untwisting the paperclip, asks from the white leather sofa.

"I didn't say it was an event." Abe makes a flailing and mopey gesture. "I just said that you could see it."

Isaac is silent because Paul O'Neill is at the plate. Awaiting the pitch, the ballplayer, with his front leg pulled in, resembles a Doberman being taunted by someone on the other side of a glass door. The pitch comes. Paul O'Neill swings and hits a pop-up and, tossing the bat, lowers his head. A scolded dog.

Isaac's face, before the small TV, is open and quiet. Justin simply can't get over it: Isaac, this subtle celebrity, is his best friend. The high school junior on that network show, the daughter of the downtown painter, and the chicest thing in all of the Dalton school, if you ask Justin, is that Isaac is the son of Diane, the rabbi of Temple Emanu-El.

Earlier this very evening Diane made a baller roasted chicken with onions like melted bulbs of glass and her tits were high and full under a red turtleneck. She has a dimple, and her brown eyes are soft, but sharp in the middle, like her pale son's own. A couple of hours ago Diane and her husband Tom disappeared into the back bedroom where Tom's sunburnt acoustic is mounted on the far wall. Tom has a ready, warm smile and a dark beard that moves with it.

The paperclip is now fully untwisted. Holding it, Justin tries to imagine what it would be like to have sex with Diane. Like napping inside of her dimple? Or like the time Kelly O'Conner intentionally grazed his dick in the bus with no air conditioning? If Justin barged into Diane and Tom's bedroom—if he said, *I'm really sorry, I have a dire medical condition that means I have to suck on Diane's juicy tits, or else I will die*, something would probably happen.

"Are we just gonna watch the Yankees all night?" Justin says.

The paper clip makes a hash mark against Justin's skin where it is callused and pink. He depresses his pink coarse skin with the stupid paper clip again, drawing blood. It's kind of nice. He feels like someone who is working on a project.

At the last sleepover when it was just Justin and Isaac and Justin lay on the trundle bed on the floor of Isaac's room and was staring into the dark bookshelf and said to Isaac what had happened with the knife, Isaac got very quiet and almost kind of dense and Justin felt wonderful, though it's also true that in that moment Justin did sort of lie because he told Isaac that the thing with the knife had happened all the time when it was only once and only a little. Even so, none of that felt dishonest. It felt like a gate was opening through which a momentous truth would come, like stretching your mouth for a new kind of kiss.

"If we were at my place, we could watch *True Lies* on LaserDisc," Abe says.

"Given that we're not there," Justin retorts. "I don't see the relevancy of that observation."

"I'm happy to watch the game," Isaac says. Bernie Williams is now at the plate. A gazelle.

Next weekend there will be Margot Levy's bat mitzvah at the Rainbow Room. That will be boring too, but at least a bitter magician with a salt-and-pepper goatee will be doing insanely good tricks behind one of those high cocktail tables. And the city's lights will shine like an orbit of stars below. Julie Stein did even imply that Justin could feel her up on the dance floor, maybe, or in some cold stairwell like had happened at Aaron Richter's bar mitzvah.

Justin spots Diane's keys on the table by the door. They are homey, fat, and fecund. Really, they look like something that ought to go in a fruit bowl. That's it! Yes! What has to happen occurs to Justin, and the boredom at the heart of the Rainbow Room, and the boredom at the heart of all the bar and bat mitzvahs that weigh on the calendar like a future of dead plants will be eradicated by the radiance of his idea!

"Let's sneak into the synagogue."

"What?" says Abe.

"What else are we going to do?"

Isaac doesn't turn from the television.

"I'm serious," Justin says.

"That's a stupid idea," Isaac says.

"More stupid, on the level of idea, than baseball?" Justin says.

"It's not gonna happen," Isaac says.

"You guys are pussies," Justin says.

When the other two say nothing, Justin throws the paperclip harder than he meant to.

"Come on," Justin says. "I want to see what it's like when it's empty."

Isaac shakes his head. He looks like Paul O'Neill when he popped out.

"Look at this shit." Justin stands and shows his bleeding finger to Isaac. The finger looks worse than it is, or maybe just as exactly bad as it feels. "Come on."

Justin swears he has magic powers: By the sheer fact of his mood, Isaac is fetching Reeboks, and Abe his New Balances. Yes! the trumpets of the band will shine like honey and the cold hunks of chocolate cake will sit on dessert plates when Justin tells Julie Cohen while feeling her up about the time he snuck into Temple Emanu-El at midnight on a Saturday…

The boys are in the mirrored, beige, rocking elevator in the Yorkville Apartment building. Isaac gives a swift and anguished nod to the cool doorman Juan who Justin once saw a hot Dominican girl wave to from an ugly lime convertible.

77th is quiet. The boys walk from York to First, from First to Second. Park Avenue, when they arrive there, is like a closed department store, with each doorman pacing in his own bright kiosk.

Isaac walks ahead. His pissy silence actually puts Justin at ease. It was also like that last December when in Miami on family vacation Justin lifted his aunt's pearl earring from where it lay on the blue and white towel and threw it in a trash can on the boardwalk. No one could prove it was him, and his cruel mother glared at Justin from within her black one-piece bathing suit, and from behind her dark and sparkling eyes. And Justin felt so free on the beach and in the salty ocean there…

After turning on to 75th, the boys arrive at the hideous exterior of Temple Emanu-El. The architecture is modern or something. A mosaic of blue and white glass props up a thick lip of concrete. The sight of the building at this odd hour helps Justin imagine that he is some kind of vandal or else an anti-Semite of the kind he is always being warned about by his grandfather and that shy, bald teacher from Hebrew School even though Justin has never met a single such person in all of his thirteen years.

These stupid little Jews! Justin thinks gleefully, picturing the temple packed with brats in black satin yarmulkes inscribed to commemorate a three-day bar spectacle tricked out with the New York Knicks City Dancers and a tacky photo booth with a green screen. How good it would feel to smash his hand through the stupid glass, how close it would be to gliding over the whole of the Earth!

Isaac struggles with the lock.

"C'mon, man," Justin says.

"There are, like, a thousand fucking keys," Isaac says. Then, like that, the lock gives.

In the stone entryway, the echoes of their footsteps flat, Isaac opens another lock, and the boys are inside. Isaac, with his hand, searches out the panel of lights. The lights come on. A red carpet leads up a flight of stairs where at Jason Ross' bar mitzvah red balloons were. Isaac opens the high wooden door to the sanctuary.

Justin and Abe follow him in. It is exciting to be there. Cold. It smells like a damp cave. And then Justin sees them: pterodactyls in the synagogue, in front of stained glass. Brown beaks, horizontal heads. Talons grip the beams. One, a great big one, flies across the sanctuary. Its leathery wings make a huge chopping sound and a shadow, like the symbol of the Batman, splashes against the floor of the temple.

Abe stays by the door. More of these tremendous creatures are on the other side, where Isaac stands. Inside the bimah Justin can see baby pterodactyls and whole families of pterodactyls resting a huge quilt of skin and bone upon a meadow of light…

On the walk back it feels close to dawn, but it is still only dark. Isaac strides ahead. All three boys are quiet. Justin couldn't tell you how long they stayed. In fact, Justin knows, beyond a doubt, he will never tell anyone what they have seen.

Kiss

Malcolm sneaks into the family room
to see if the video is on.
In the one that is his favorite,
Prince is a man
who wears leather pants and no shirt,
and there is a veiled dancer
with a black choker that is crowned
with white crystal heart.

The one other time Malcom saw the video,
it was obvious to him
the dancer didn't pirouette
in the way Prince would
if her body was his.

That time, also, the whole front
of the coffee table turned red
while the kingdom of the song
draped itself over the room.

But none of that is what's important,
which has to do with the woman
in the streaked jumpsuit with shoulder pads
who is the guitarist.

What happens is
Prince leans his face rudely close
to the face of this woman, like he might as well be sticking
his dirty undies there
while singing about the fact
the woman who will deserve his kiss
can't talk dirty.

That is what
Malcolm is here
to see: the moment
the woman's scrunched nose
turns into a smile.

He pictures it
all the time.

Tapping his foot on the school bus,
imagining the aisle were red,
Malcolm recalls the smiling woman's
revoked disgust while Prince fusses
with the knobs of the music machine.

Movies

Don't Worry, He Won't Get Far On Foot

Corky is telling her story to a roomful of addicts.
She has never experienced anguish unless boredom
is a kind of it, she says, about having run naked
through the suburbs. A porcelain statue of Rococo
dancers stands on a table as a witness to her tale.

Jonah Hill attends the meeting because he is the leader,
and this is his house. He is gay.
He has gorgeous golden locks.
His anger is like a greyhound,
and his love is the camera that runs along the track
filming the animal.

Later comes Joaquin Phoenix who occupies a wheelchair
with a smile of temporary ecstatic okness.

Phoenix plays John Callahan, a cartoonist who's quadriplegic
due to alcohol.

The figures in Callahan's cartoons are bug-eyed skeins,
and the cartoonist's jokes report from a rolling green
—a land called Universal Humiliation—
where families from different neighborhoods can picnic together.

The film has styles:
camp, drama, porno, love.

Jonah Hill is at last dying from AIDS
in a way that is stolid and intense
when he says to Joaquin Phoenix,

I've tried to teach people faith,
and Phoenix with the bursting passion of a person who is not good
    with words
hugs Hill enormously, and it is moving because it is true
that faith is like tastelessness.

Nocturnal Animals

The gallerist wears a black jade to the opening. She is putting
    on a show.
Obese nudes in giant installations shake pompoms in front of
    the red curtains.
Sculptures of the white and rippling women also lie on plinths,
like downed animals.

"The new work is strong," a friend in a designer purple silk coat assures
the gallerist, who remains lost
in front of art.

The gallerist is Amy Adams.
She lives on the verge of tears under eyeliner walls.

In a photograph in her mansion of steel and glass,
a man in a trucker hat points a rifle at another man,
who grins at the viewer.

And an installation holds suspended with steel cables, a dead steer
shot through with arrows
in a tank of blue formaldehyde.

Because he was weak, the gallerist's mother, in three layers of pearls,
did warn her daughter not to marry the man
who sends the manuscript
the gallerist lingers over

from languorous positions
inside her modernist abode.

In the novel, a beautiful killer swims through evil
like a dolphin in jeans, and the redheaded wife
and the daughter, whom the killer disposes of, lie fair
and naked on a sofa in a junkyard in West Texas,
with tires rising behind them like so much smoke.

Disturbed by the image words have suggested,
the gallerist phones her own child,
and the redheaded beauty answers from a black bed,

where she and a lover lie
in the way
the corpses did.

Fwiw I can prove (in a paper I am working on)
that the rich who bulldoze beauty and pay each other huzzahs
will be forgotten like breath, and the lucre they love
does not know their name.

They Live

It is a world of jack hammers and exploding helicopters
and fitness instructors on the television in sheer nylon with their hair
    in a bun…

The two men are ok in a homeless encampment.
They have traveled in the veined and jagged itineraries that hide
in the shadows of a corporate decade.

One of the men is strong and Black with a rich and mellifluous voice.

The other is white, with the neck of a hedgehog, and is the
    professional wrestler
Rowdy Roddy Piper.

Each man hates when the other walks behind him,
so they are friends.

In the basement of a church, the wrestler discovers
a bin of sunglasses as juicy as blackberries.
Many good and nervous people have been going
in and out of that holy building:
a blind priest and a man in the beige kind of vest
that has many pockets.

Putting on the glasses, the wrestler sees
what's up.

But Rowdy Roddy Piper needs also for his friend to know.
But the friend will not do it. He won't put the glasses on.
And in the alley the two go at it
with the noise of the trucks on either side
in the gauntlet of thick and ancient graffiti.

They fight for so long.
Time gets weird
as they dispense with their friendship
in order to be comrades in arms.

Where Is the Friend's House?

The classroom of the village schoolhouse has a scored door with no lock.
The schoolboys chirp like cuckoo birds.
When the teacher arrives late, in a parka,

he berates the students. A blond body has forgotten
his notebook again. A third time: expulsion.

Hearing the teacher's threats,
the boy cries. His tears never find
the adult hand that hears them.
His pain, though, is witnessed
by a boy with dark spiky hair
whose name is Ali.

Over a basin in a dusty courtyard
Ali's mother screams at her son
about a slew of chores
when he comes home. A moment later,
after he has made the awful
discovery, Ali attempts to explain
the mistake to his mother, but language
gets him nowhere.

In this hamlet
words are shoves
dished out among people
who are tied
to one another.

So what, the stupid kid deserves
to be expelled
even if you took his notebook
by mistake, Ali's mother yells, throwing a bottle
at her uppity son.

What can he do? The question tosses
in the boy's tormented eye.
Then he is off on a lonely adventure

in the green and brown villages
where no one can listen or see.

When Ali comes home, an astonishing
gust throws open the gate,
as he copies out the homework
for his dear classmate, his friend
whose house he could not find.

Desert Surface #1

A month after the last time I ever saw you
I ended up going
to a retrospective at the Met Breuer
of the work of the artist Vija Celmins.

You may not know that in the 1960s
Celmins walked every day
to the pier at Venice Beach
and took a photograph of the ocean
and then made pencil drawings
of some of the photographs she took.

The drawings of the ocean were in the first room
at the Met Breuer
the day that I went there.

Of course, all of this made me think of you.

That afternoon in Malibu, you were making your watercolor
of the ocean. Boy, that was some vacation.
Whenever I tried to touch you,
you screamed at a ghost above my shoulder.
My needs, like teeth, were finally coming in.

In Malibu, fat lavender shadows lay in ruffled folds
under the pier where I had wandered
out of a conscious effort to give you space.
I went past wet black rocks and a sandy hollow
where two surfers in sweatshirts shared a bowl.

Earlier that day, at the Getty, when I was weeping
over my $25 chicken salad,

I was thinking about how disregarded
you had felt
in your own life. And on the hike
down from the museum, the slithered pockets
of my subtle body
burned with little fires
I wished for you to pat out.

Every minute on that trip I learned so much
and was so unhappy.

That afternoon in Malibu you wanted
to go to the exact beach
where you had previously had
a magical experience
filming a video.

The dolphins had surfaced
out of sparkling water, you said.

I was happy to drive.

We were in and out of service but did eventually
find the place.

It was cloudy and sharply gray and then sunny.

The watercolor you made
was not very good.

I didn't think any of your art was.

You had to let irony in.
You had to be less proud.

I do have a habit
of being ingratiating
when I'm angry. I think
I'm less like that now.

I really wanted to text you
from in front of Celmins' work.

At the Met that day, a woman wore a black leather jacket
over a tangerine dress,
and there were several cloth totes
marked by the serifed names of magazines.

The exhibit showed Celmins' drawings
of the moon and spider webs and stars
as well as small sculptures she had made
of eleven rocks
that are identical
to eleven real rocks.

You would have found her art beautiful.

The whole time I was imagining
walking there with you
in the kind of secrecy we could enjoy
inside a place that is ruled by silence.

I read about Celmins after the show.
And one thing that stood out
is that she enjoys
using the word "dumb"
to recall the subjects
of the earliest of her own work
that she considers good,

which are these plain,
but haunted, paintings of everyday objects
that happened to be lying around her studio
in Venice Bench in 1964.

A hotpot, a heater, two white lamps.
That kind of thing.

I also read a *New Yorker* profile
that gave a partial catalogue
of Celmins' apparently numerous pets:
an Alaskan malamute, a Shiba Inu, and
a black cat called Raymond,

which stood out, too,
because I could picture Celmins hugging Raymond close to her,
the way you would hug Daphne and Melanie so close to you
and call them dumb,
and sometimes even shove them off the bed
in a way you claimed their mothers did.

In museums we get to be pets
when we look
at the ones
people have made.

I did try to use my looking
to make you mine,
and I am sorry about that,

but I still believe
you treated me
poorly.

I used to want for others
to go outside and come back
to the hushed and lonely
style of place
where I tend to reside, draped
in stories about the stars and sea.

Now I wear a surface and go out.

The Glass-Bottom Boat

The woman whose face was as soft
and white as homemade paper
summoned me to the banquette
because I could not hide that I was a listener.

She had once been a model,
she told me that night fifteen years ago
at the bar on 6th Street
where nothing ever happened.

The story she had to tell
had to do with a builder of motorcycles.
He's a painter, too, she said.
His show is ten minutes from here.

I used to have
nowhere to go.

The exhibit was in a big, bright room divided by particle boards
and people ambled amid the broad fluorescence,
wearing shearling coats and trucker hats.
On the walk over, I had imagined a flannel shirt bulging
with a pack of Marlboro Reds. But the painter wore an Oakland A's
    cap pulled low
over the rat-like face of a roadie. My new acquaintance
laid a hand to the chest of her open white blouse
while pleading with the grim and shadowed man.

I left soon after that.

I had forgotten all of this
until maybe a year ago

when I was being provided for
inside the Glass-Bottom Boat
doing cognitive labor
for an oligarch I met
at a chess tournament
in Alaska, and whose name
you would probably know.

Ok, sure. For many years
I wished to have a pointy face
women smash themselves upon
like bottles
against a ship's prow.

But just as much
I longed to wear eye shadow
and tell of my suffering
until an obedient child came
to hear each note.

If I exercise my mind
using our proprietary method,
I can hear them still:
The former model is pattering through
the Louvre, at two a.m.,
in a hall wrecked with moonlight,
and the painter is in Hudson, NY,
giving his Pilates instructor wife
the silent treatment…

But there I go again.
Even in the best gigs
we trade on our faults.

God is Sexting Me

From a hole
in the mind the
fangs of years
tore open, a
signal comes…

I am blessed.
I am blessed.
God is sexting me.

To Denis Johnson

In a video I've seen on YouTube,
you're standing in a classroom in a flannel shirt.

You are talking about plays,
which you wrote many of,
apparently.

The subject appears
to make you jocular
and frightened.

You don't understand plays,
and don't understand why you like writing them;

what you are saying about playwriting
isn't what you believe,
I conclude when
watching this clip.

I tend to pair you with Nabokov
because of a kind of crypto timidity;
though in Nabokov's case, this
shyness was tucked behind walls
of snootiness, whereas you turned yours
inside out
through spasmodic means.

And Nabokov could, after all, enjoy
the pleasures of the polymath, the wistfulness of the émigré,
and you were a junkie, and your father was CIA.
But still, in my book,
you are two chronophobiacs, two peas
in a pod…

You were drawn to failed lands,
where authority had come loose,
in order to sneak up on your father's face,
which rose shadowed and locked into one direction,
like one of those Easter Island deals…

The truth to you felt
like the light that comes
off a prison tower.

In a photo I've seen,
you are smiling in a chair and wearing sunglasses,
sitting on uneven concrete
in a church parking lot, maybe,

and the joys of an unsewn heart
are held together in the face
of you in the chair smiling
as the fire over your shoulder
burns.

What a photo!

It makes me want
to congratulate you.

Aaron Judge

The bat he swings is like a horse
rearing ahead of the charioteer,
carrying the man
in a regal and statuesque roar
off the ground.

When the right fielder trots around
that shell in the Bronx,
he keeps his head down.

He measures the bounce
and throws out the runner
lunging for second. Getting his man,
he is pleased. His smile washes in like the tide.

The commentators go on about your money,
    rubbing their hands, killing time.
Aaron, it's ok:
you are good enough!

Blind Spot

New Year's, 2010. On top of the sink,
in the bathroom of that stranger's loft.
The countdown had already begun
in a boozy chorus behind the door.
You shimmied
and thumbed down
the band of your black tube top.
The petals of light in your eyes,
reflected in the silver mirror,
looked like taut jump ropes...

I used to leap at the chance
to be ensconced in someone
who was somewhere else.
We were joined by that wish,
like when I came so far
down your throat
that you could not taste it.

Abundance

That store of wealth, the perfect place:
Scrooge McDuck splashing
in his sacred money bin!

These lowlifes who had busted out of jail
with the prison numbers still
appended to their clothes
because of an enduring criminal nature
were called the Beagle Boys.

A bunch of nitwits.
God had granted them
a single dream: to drain the safe
ringed with stitched steel
the blissful curmudgeon swam in
for whole afternoons,
bathed from bill to toe
in coins of gold.

Poodles? Chew toys?
What would those creeps
have made of that abundance,
the best use of which
Scrooge had found?

Samantha, the Dentist

At the dive bar with a nautical theme
that I went to on friend's suggestion,
she was to be found by the wagging taps—
her hair like hay in blazing July.

Thank God I sat.
I had been so foolish and afraid!

So the rumors are true:
a healthy mouth can contribute
to a healthy heart.

The Bach on our Sonos is a golden Koi.

Our hardwood palace is almost entirely wireless.

I am worthy, I am worthy.
I am in love with Samantha, the dentist.

To Albert Ayler

In interviews you have a soft and rapt voice,
like that of a novitiate
staring at a flame.

I read you are believed
to have felt responsible
for the suffering
of your brother, Donald,
who had a psychotic break
after you convinced him to move to New York
for your band,

and that you and your band would go
three or four days without food
because no one in New York
understood your music.

I was very lonely when I discovered your music,
and happy. I was sleeping
in this roomy culvert
with a view of a lake,
and had an old Sony boom box,
on which I played a tape
of "Zion Hill" again and again
until squirrels
and even once an armadillo
came around.

You helped keep me
in that kosher place.

I listened to the recording of you

at John Coltrane's funeral,
where you appeared at his dying request.
In the photo of that performance,
you are in a white suit,
the rest of the band in black.

The recording is crummy,
but you can be heard
crying out —

the way a candle is intolerant
of the darkness around
its little cowl,
your notes are just as intolerant
of lies.

Hearing that recording
from the balcony of St. Peter's,
I think, what if Icarus went
all the way up
and called down, Hey, Dad,
forget the labyrinth and the sea,
we can live here.

Bartleby's Diet

Probably a single glass of milk made a trip
across the planed surfaces
of a boarding house's upper room,
leaving behind the rings
of a private galaxy.

Or was it seventy-five
thousand boiled eggs?

What sustained you?

Herring sourced
amid the pealing bells
of South Street Seaport
under a gulled November sky?

Could you have been found
behind a chessboard of waiters
in the corner of a diner,
blowing on vegetable soup,

whispering your favorite prayer
before taking in
the closest thing
you could find to food?

Pebbled Lips

"I'm a pescatarian only because I hate fish,"
she said. She had arrived twelve minutes late
to the jazz club on Greenville that is no longer there.
As if smudged with Vaseline,
her eyes lived in a wild, cloudy, summery blur.
She wore a blue wool coat and a leather skirt.
A little piece of her blond eyebrow was missing.

Later, excusing herself, she grabbed her clutch
and walked to the bathroom in a choppy strut
followed by a gossipy retinue of self-consciousness.

Against her Saab in the windy lot
her soft hair brushed against my neck.
She smiled at me with big, blue, foggy eyes.

In New York, during my break,
I visited a jewelry shop on Elizabeth Street.
An egret-necked man in a cape
pointed to chunky fruits of stone
under glass: Black Apache, amethyst, and jade.
The prices were told in elegant cursive.

I would bite into that jade and kiss her collarbone
with pebbled lips…

I would saunter into the future
with the silhouette
of that price tag…

When we slept side by side,
my dreams were hers.

Once I met two girls
who wore dirty silk nightgowns
and lived in a house with blackened windows.
The little one was sweet,
but the tall one could make a single rotten face at me…

Even now, in Wednesday traffic,
when the Baghdad of Dallas
pours itself to the horizon,
there is a window in the air,
and I see them, my charges,
from afar, as faraway as stars.

Nick in the Video Room

The Video Room
is where I see you
facing the screaming buses.

Death must be a pimp
in a sexploitation flick
and you're one of his captives now.
Or something. On your lip
there is a notch of cleft flesh.

In the window float
coughing reflections
of passersby, and the
black and red VHS cassettes
are kept in neat little tiers.

When I go
behind the counter
to where you wait for me,
your style is rather impersonal.

In the backroom
a gray sweatshirt has fallen
over a swivel chair,
and there is that vault
you are leaning over.

It is a place the living
don't normally go.

Like a projector being fed
the thin insect-iridescent roll of film
is what it is like
when the hot celluloid
melts on my tongue.

To Pema Chodron

During my years
in Midtown East,
I liked to watch
your interviews.

In the city of rushing sleepwalkers,

the expressions on your face changed at such a truthful rate,

and the kernels of laughter
detonated
from the back of your throat
like popcorn.

You talked about the moment
your husband pulled up
to leave you in New Mexico:

the beginning of your turning
into a nun.

Everything
you said
was spinning.

When my friend drove his Saturn into a tree,

and when he and I
would hang out
after,
in the style of two lovers
who are both independently awake at 4 a.m., I was inside the place

your books

come from.

Your writing's like this bone I saw
in a Celtics game.

A player fell

and the femur
went through.

The whole game had to stop.

Double Indemnity

Yesterday
I walked
to where
a tree leaned over the creek.

Wyoming is the real deal.

The light
is like a loofah.

It's def weird working for a guy
I know almost only
from all-lowercase emails and clips
on the internet
where he mutters about
the economy in a blue Patagonia vest,

but I'm left alone.

And when I stare through
the soles of my feet,
the guides hold my lungs
in the calipers of their fingers,

and being so
mortal and connected,
I think of you,

my dear friend,
as you start
your adventure.

Your close family used their brooms
to sweep away
ten of your years,
and when gaps appear
in a friend's smile,
anger bleeds through
your chest
like a sunrise.

But all the stuff
with your sister
is only natural
if you are to stand
under your own bright star.

I'm pretty busy these days
seeking the distance
from which I can access
all of my love,

and the movie I want
to recommend
is *Double Indemnity*,
which is
my favorite film.

It's about an insurance man named Walter Neff.

At the beginning of the movie, he visits a Spanish-style home
called the Dietrichson residence.
At the head of the stairs appears this woman Phyllis,
who wears only a gold anklet and a towel.

This hot, cruel stranger sends Neff to wait
in a dark living room. The slatted daylight streams in
through Venetian blinds, and on a side table there is a photo
of a man and a girl the salesman consults
in an idle and masculine way.

Motes thicken the close air.

The whole thing is told in a voice-over by Neff,
who has been shot and is confessing
into the dictagraph
of his revered colleague, Keyes.

Because he can't stop remembering the anklet,
the salesman returns to the house,
which is when Phyllis happens to ask
if there is a way
her boorish life partner
could sign up for accident insurance
without his knowing.

Neff leaves at once and goes to a drive-in joint
where the waiters wear hats made out of folded white paper. And he
    bowls.
He returns to his bachelor pad that has on its walls the lithographs of
    boxers.

It is a rainy night, and the rain makes the light wavy.

When Phyllis knocks
on his door,
Neff lets her in.

The salesman tries to convince her not to do it
in such a querulous way.

His face is a tiny dark cathedral.

This is exactly
what Neff says:

Maybe she had stopped thinking about it [the proposed murder],
but I hadn't. I couldn't. Because it all tied up with something I had
been thinking about for years, since long before I ever ran into Phyllis
Dietrichson. Because, in this business, you can't sleep for trying
to figure out the tricks they could pull on you. You're like the guy
behind the roulette wheel, watching the customers to make sure they
don't crook the house. And then one night, you get to thinking how
you could crook the house yourself. And do it smart. Because you've
got that wheel right under your hands. And you know every notch in
it by heart. And you figure all you need is a plant out in front, a shill
to put down the bet. And suddenly the doorbell rings and the whole
set-up is right there in the room with you...

And there's this other, later, crucial moment
when Keyes has determined that a man falling
off a train going 15 mph
would have a very hard time breaking his neck,

and Neff sneaks into the assessor's office to eavesdrop
on the tapes Keyes does his special thinking into. On one of these reels,
Keyes says in response
to a higher-up's suspicion:

...I've known Walter Neff intimately for eleven years
and personally vouch for him
without reservation...

If only the salesman could have heard these words sooner,
he would not have had to chase the astonishing rewards

of an extreme insurance, I think, watching Neff
receive this beautiful and inapt assessment.

But no.

What happens is,
is that Phyllis is evil,

and Neff transfers his affections
to Lola, the girl
whose father he has strangulated
to death and then
passed himself off as while tumbling off
the back of a train.

Neff and the girl go around the dark city.
They picnic in these small, haunted woods above the Hollywood Bowl.

Lola is a fount of the same light
that is in Keyes,
but in a less rigid form,

and the crooked
strands in Neff

are held in her eyes

like flowers in a fist.

Neff has found the innocent,

but only

by tying a short rope around Mr. Dietrichson's neck

and pulling it as hard
as Neff could from the cold back
of the now-dead man's automobile.

And that is why I am recommending
this film to you,
my brave pal:

Even as
he bleeds
at dawn,

Neff
isn't wasting his time

because

the man has met

his original face,

and that can't be done without
a trip across

a lonely corridor

lined with

what is so

like killing.

Outside the government
of family,

the expressions
we have worn

can fall away

in

the Venetian light

of

a luminous corner.

Have faith.

You have a hidden
friend who
loves you.

NOTES

The use of "slithered" to describe pockets in "Desert Surface #1" is taken from Hart Crane's "Chaplinesque."

"Oedipus at Colonus" uses a quotation from Robert Fitzgerald's translation of *Oedipus at Colonus*.

"Double Indemnity" includes quotations from Billy Wilder and Raymond Chandler's screenplay for the film *Double Indemnity*.

ACKNOWLEDGMENTS

This book would not have been completed without the friendship and editorial assistance of Gemma Sieff. I thank my pal Greg Brownderville for his help and guidance. I am grateful to Kyle McCord and Gold Wake Press, and to Elijah Burrell, for his close and thoughtful edits. I thank Rick Bozorth and Tom DiPiero, and all of my generous colleagues at Southern Methodist University. I thank my agent, Jin Auh, and the Wylie Agency; and my parents, Beverly and Jeffrey Rubin, for their loving support.

ABOUT THE AUTHOR

Jacob Rubin is an assistant professor of English at Southern Methodist University. The author of the novel *The Poser*, he lives in Dallas, Texas.

www.ingramcontent.com/pod-product-compliance
Lightning Source LLC
Chambersburg PA
CBHW021131080526
44587CB00012B/1234